To:_____

From:_____

Date:_____

The God Questions
Exploring Life's Great Questions About God

Hal Seed

Table of Contents

CONTENTS

Introduction

INTRODUCTION

Nothing can stabilize this vast and shifting world like solid, sensible answers about the God who made it.

In the back of my mind, I have questions about God. *"Is He real?" "Can He be trusted?" "Is there really a heaven, and am I on a path to get there?"* Years ago, I decided to do an "Ask the Audience" kind of series with the church I lead. I drew up a simple survey that said, "If you could ask God any question, what would it be?" To my surprise, everyone filled out that survey. Many wrote multiple questions. Some asked if they could submit questions their neighbors were asking.

From that simple survey, I learned that **everyone has questions about God.**

Maybe you feel like your questions are unanswerable. A few of them might be ("Can God build a structure so weighty that not even He can lift it?"), but most of the questions that really trouble us are questions God really wants to answer for us. God made us intelligent, reasoning beings. When it comes to faith and the spiritual realm, He doesn't expect us to leave our brains at the door. He wants us to think deeply and, as much as we are able, understand Him and His ways.

I'm one of those people who needs answers. Maybe you are, too. Before I enter a contest, I want to know how the thing works. Before I invest time or money, I need to know if the plan makes sense. Before I can recommend a product, I have to know its purpose and see if it actually does what it claims to do. Until the pieces fit together for me, the unknown can be unappealing at best, and big and confusing at worst. In my experience, nothing can stabilize this vast and shifting world like solid, sensible answers about the God who made it.

That's what *The God Questions* is all about. I hope (and believe) that some of what you read in this condensed version will surprise you. I pray that it will change you and, in a spiritual sense, set you free.

I have repeated my "God Survey" several times over the past fifteen years. From it, I've discovered that there are really four major questions people ask about God: *"Is He real?" "Is the Bible true?" "What about other religions?" "Why does He allow suffering?"* In this condensed version of *The God Questions*, I hope to give you enough answers about God to stabilize your world.

Is God Real?

IS GOD REAL?

*"The first question which should rightly be asked is:
Why is there something rather than nothing?"*
G. W. Leibniz

Throughout human history, people have questioned the existence of God. We can't see, hear, feel, touch or taste Him, so how can we know for sure if He exists?

This is such an important question that scholars have given it deep thought over the ages. Many have concluded that God must be real, and there are sound reasons to believe in Him. I'd like to give you five of them. Together, these five reasons form a compelling argument that God is real. They'll even point you toward the kind of God He is.

Reason #1—The Universe

The universe itself is a powerful pointer to the existence of God. It's big and beautiful, and all of its parts work together well. Its very existence raises the question: *"How did the universe get here?"*

Answering that question has led many scientists and philosophers to conclude that God must exist.

Think about it: If nothing existed, would you have to explain it? Of course not! But the moment something exists, it raises the question, "How did this thing get here?"

The obvious answer is, "It came from something else." Animals came from their parents, plants came from seeds, houses came from a builder and cars came from factories. Everything comes from something else. Everything in the universe is **contingent** on something that came before it.

What's more, everything is **dependent** on something else for its existence. Humans depend on food to live. Plants depend on the sun for photosynthesis. The sun depends on gravity to keep from breaking apart. So everything in the universe seems to have come from something else, and everything in the universe seems to be dependent on something else for its existence.

Push way back into the history of the universe and ask, "Where did all of this stuff come from?" The answer most people come to is "God". Everything in the universe was created by something else and depends on something else. The cause of all of this must be something that is uncreated and independent—or, in positive terms, something that is **eternal** and **self-sufficient**. The only being that could fit such a description is God.

Another way to think about this is to view the universe as one big object. Using your mind as a camera lens, zoom out so far that you capture everything in the universe in this circle:

THE UNIVERSE

Everything inside the circle is contingent and dependent.

The universe has not always existed. Therefore, it must have come from something that is non-contingent and non-dependent. Those two terms come very close to a working definition of God.

The Bible says "*...the heavens declare the glory of God; the skies proclaim the work of his hands... There is no speech or language where their voice is not heard. Their voice goes out into all the earth, their words to the end of the world.*" (Psalm 19:1).

God is communicating to us through what we see of the universe! He's saying, "I am here. I exist. You can tell, because I made this place."

Everything that's been made must have a maker. The French skeptic Voltaire once said, "I shall always be convinced that a watch proves a watch-maker." In the same way, the existence of the universe proves a God.

Reason #2—The Creator

My wife and I have a very special box in a cabinet in our garage. It contains scores of pictures our daughter Amy drew as a little girl. If you look through the box, you can guess how old Amy was at the painting of each

10

picture. Some look like they were painted by a four-year-old, others by an eight-year-old, still others by a sixteen-year-old. You can tell a lot about a creator by studying what she (or he) has created.

That's the gist of the second evidence for the existence of God. The rationale goes like this: **every design reflects its designer.**

Chart the path of the stars, measure the decay rate of an atom, examine the laws of physics; everything you can study is well-ordered, precise and complex. Stare up into the night sky, walk along a beach at sunset, put a snowflake under a microscope; everywhere you look, our world is saturated with beauty. These are pointers not only to a Creator, but also to the nature of the Creator: ingenious, beautiful and detailed.

The beauty and complexity of the universe point not only to a God, but hint at what kind of God He must be.

Plato decided that it was reasonable to believe in God based on "the order of the motion of the stars, and of all things under the dominion of the mind which ordered the universe."[1] Sir Isaac Newton said, "When I look at the solar system, I see the earth at the right distance from the sun to receive the proper amounts of heat and light. This did not happen by chance."[2]

The Pepsi Can[3]

Imagine sitting on the desk in front of you is a Pepsi can. How did it get there?

Here's a theory: Millennia ago, a huge explosion sent a small meteor spinning through space. As it cooled, a caramel-colored, effervescent liquid formed on its surface. As time passed, aluminum crept out of the water and shaped itself into just these dimensions. Over time, this thing formed itself a one-time retractable lid from which a crease appeared, a bit off-center, and out of it grew a pull-tab. Centuries later, red, white, and blue paint fell from the sky and clung to its exterior, forming the letters P-e-p-s-i on its surface. This Pepsi can fits perfectly in the palm of the normal-sized human hand. Its volume is just about right for satisfying one person's desire for something sweet and liquid. It has just enough caffeine to pep you up, but not so much that you realize you're actually in an artificially induced state of stimulation. Its contents are always the same. Its quality never varies.

How many scientific explanations about the nature of matter and the origins of the universe would I have to give to convince you that the Pepsi can happened by chance? What are the odds that something this complex, useful, comfortable and attractive came about as a result of a random collision of molecules? The can is too carefully designed to have been formed by chance or coincidence. Some very smart people did some careful thinking and planning to create it.

The Banana

Now, hold a banana in your hand.

The banana fits perfectly in your palm. In fact, it fits better than the Pepsi can. It's been thoughtfully made with a non-slip surface. It comes with a time-sensitive indicator on the outside to let you know the condition of the contents before you even open it: green means, "keep going," yellow means, "slow down and eat it," black means, "too late, friend."

The banana's top contains a pull-tab for convenient opening. Pull back firmly on the tab, and it peels neatly according to its pre-made perforations. If it's at just the right stage for eating, it even gives off a little "click" sound as it's opened. The wrapper peels into four pieces and hangs gracefully over your hand. Unlike the Pepsi can, this wrapper is environmentally sensitive, made completely of bio-degradable substances that in time enrich the soil it nestles in. If left uneaten, it has pre-programmed orders to reproduce itself into a whole new fruit-bearing plant, so it is a virtually inexhaustible food-producing source.

The fruit is the perfect size and shape for the human mouth, with a point on the top for easy entry. It is full of bodybuilding calories and is easy for the stomach to digest. And the Maker-of-the-banana has even curved it toward the face to make the whole eating experience easier and more pleasant.

No wonder the Bible says about God, *"Your workmanship is marvelous..."*[4] From looking at the design of the banana, I conclude that there is a God; that He is brilliant, creative and thoughtful; and that He loves to delight people through all five of our senses.

Reason #3—Our Sense of Morality

Everyone has morals. No one obeys them fully.

Having moral standards that are higher than our ability to keep them points toward a **Moral Standard-Giver**.

When I was a small child, my mother and I had a tradition. We would go to the store together, and if I was a good boy, she would buy me a treat. One of the saddest days of my young life was the day that didn't happen. I remember it vividly. We were standing in the checkout line, and I put my candy bar on the conveyor belt.

"No," she said, "I'm not buying you a treat today."

"Why not? I've been a good boy."

"I'm just not, that's all."

Since she had no good reason *not* to get me the candy bar, I saw no good reason not to get it for myself. I pretended to take it back to the candy aisle, but on the way I buried it deep in my pants pocket.

Can you guess why I remember that day so vividly? Yep, I got caught.

"What are you eating?" Mom asked.

"A candy bar."

"And where did you get it?"

"At the grocery store."

"And how did you pay for it?"

"I didn't."

What followed was a lesson I will never forget. Mom drove me back to the store, located the store manager, and made me admit my theft, apologize and pay for the candy bar. I felt embarrassed, humiliated and ashamed all at the same time.

Did I learn my lesson? Yes and no. Yes, I learned that crime doesn't pay. But no, I didn't learn to be absolutely honest from that day forward. The truth is, when I took that candy bar, I knew what I was doing was wrong, but I did it anyway.

And I've done it since then. I haven't stolen any more candy bars, but I have taken things that didn't belong to me. And I've done worse. I've said things that weren't true in order to make myself look better. I've done things to other people that I knew would hurt them.

I've taken surveys in my church where I've asked, "How many of you have never said anything that you knew wasn't true or taken something that didn't belong to you?" No one has raised their hand. We're all guilty. We all have a moral standard that we believe in but can't seem to live up to.

How many times have you started to do something, and an alarm in your head said, *"Don't do that!"* but you did it anyway? How many times have you opened your mouth and your conscience said, *"Don't say it!"* but you said it anyway? You know what the right thing is, even if you don't always do it. Where did that sense of "right" come from? This is the third reason to believe in God: we all have a moral standard that is higher than we are.

Ethical codes vary from person to person and culture to culture, but every human being has an innate moral standard. Where did this moral standard come from?

Since it's impossible to invent something that is greater than we are, there is only one reasonable answer: **There is a moral Creator who put this standard in us.**

Reason #4—Jesus

One of the greatest evidences of the existence of God is the life of Jesus Christ.

Jesus claimed to be God.[5] Many people struggle with this claim, because there are only two possibilities for it: either it's true, or it's not true.

If it's true, He is Lord and God.

If it's not true, there are only two possibilities. One is, His claim was false, and He knew it. The other is, His claim was false, and He didn't know it, but actually thought He was God.

If it was false and He knew it, that would make Him a **liar**.

If it was false and He didn't know it, that would make Him a **lunatic**. (Any person who really believes he is God must be clinically insane.)

This is what's known as "The Trilemma."[6]

It presents us with three choices—Jesus was either the Lord, a liar, or a lunatic.

C.S. Lewis, who was once an avowed agnostic, saw the reasoning behind this and eventually became a Christian as a result. Afterwards, he wrote in his book *Mere Christianity*:

> A man who was merely a man and said the sort of things that Jesus said would not be a great moral teacher. He would either be a lunatic—on a level with a man who says he is a poached egg—or else he would be the Devil of Hell. You must make your choice. Either this man was, and is, the son of God: or else a madman or something worse.[7]

Mohammed and Joseph Smith claimed to be prophets. Buddha and Confucius were silent on the idea of God. Only Jesus claimed to be God in the flesh.

On Good Friday, Jesus was flogged 39 times with a cat-o-nine tails.[8] This process injured Him so badly that, by the time it was over, His flesh was in ribbons and His organs were exposed.[9] A crown of thorns was placed on His head,[10] and a 110-pound crossbar was placed on His shoulders.[11] He was too weak from the beating to make it all the way up the hill, so a bystander named Simon of Cyrene was forced to carry the crossbar for Him.[12] He was nailed to a cross, where He was pronounced dead by a professional Roman executioner, who verified His death by piercing the tissue

surrounding his heart with a spear.[13] This Centurion was so impressed with the way Jesus faced death that he remarked; "Truly this man was the Son of God!"[14]

According to Jewish custom, Jesus' body was placed on a stone table in the burial chamber (which was a freshly prepared tomb hewn out of solid rock[15]). He was washed with warm water and packed in 100 pounds of spices.[16] His body was wrapped in no fewer than three separate burial garments,[17] and a stone weighing nearly two tons was placed in front of the tomb's doorway.[18] Pontius Pilate (the Roman ruler of Judea) ordered a guard unit[19] to make the tomb "as secure as you know how."[20] The guards sealed the stone to the tomb[21] with clay packs and stamped it with Pilate's official signet ring.

From what they had witnessed, Jesus' disciples were discouraged, scared and in shock.[22] When reports of Jesus' resurrection came in, they refused to believe that He was alive.[23]

If Jesus didn't rise from the dead, His disciples would have known it. Of the original twelve disciples, Judas Iscariot hanged himself believing that his betrayal caused Jesus' death.[24] John died in exile in modern day Turkey. The other ten were all put to death for their faith. Sometimes good men will die for a good cause, but how likely is it that that many would die for a lie?

Jesus' tomb had been sealed, and the penalty for breaking a Roman seal was crucifixion upside down.[25] Who would have the courage or motivation to do this? The huge stone covering the tomb was rolled uphill to open the tomb entrance. Who would have the strength and numbers to do this? The Roman guard unit was trained to hold their ground against an entire battalion. Who could have overcome them?[26] When Mary, Peter and the others viewed the grave clothes, they were undisturbed (except the face cloth, which was rolled up in a place by itself [27]). The linen wrappings were lying on the table in the form of a body, slightly caved in and empty. How did that happen?

Five people examined the tomb and found it empty on what would become the first Easter Sunday morning.[28] Over the next 40 days,

Jesus appeared to more than 515 eyewitnesses.[29] These eyewitnesses were from various stations in life and various states of disbelief. But their lives were so changed that they, in turn, devoted the rest of their lives to sharing the story of Jesus' resurrection with as many people as they could reach. What can explain this? Only God.

Reason #5—Personal Experience

On January 20, 1971, I agreed to visit a Christian coffeehouse event with some friends. I was not a Christian at the time. On the way there, one of my friends, Dick Roth, said, "I talked to God this morning."

The idea of talking to God seemed so absurd that I laughed out loud. However, two hours later on the way home, Dick asked me if I wanted to begin a personal relationship with God. I did!

What happened to me? I had an experience with God at that coffeehouse. I saw evidence of His real presence in the lives of the people there. And I experienced His presence for myself, personally. The whole idea of having a relationship with God was so new to me that when I woke up the next morning I had to verify it. So I asked the question I've asked many times since: "God, are you really there?" As I said that, I suddenly had a sense that He was saying, "Yes, I'm here." I even felt subtle chills run down my spine. I have asked that same question hundreds of times since then, and every time I ask I get the same response: "Yes, I'm here," and I get chills. That's been happening now for 33 years.

How do I explain that?

Some might say, "Well, you just really wanted to believe." But I really didn't. I was content with my life. However, I experienced enough evidence that night to convince me that there was a God, a God who was interested in having a relationship with me. So I invited Him to be my friend and leader, and the minute I did, I experienced Him.

The Bible says that everyone can have an experience with God if they sincerely look for him. *"Ask and it will be given to you; seek and you will find; knock and the door will be opened to you."* [30] It also says that we were made to experience God. That *"God…has planted eternity in the human heart…"* [31]

What's at Stake?

Some people seem to have a strong desire to believe in God. They want assurance that they're not alone in the universe. Other people have an equally strong desire to *not* believe in God. The thought of an all-powerful Creator cramps their style.

If there really is a Creator of this universe, then it's His property. In fact, *we* are His property.

When I was a little guy, my parents built a swimming pool in our yard. Whenever the pool deck got wet, it got slippery, so my parents made a rule to keep us safe: "No running on the pool deck." The rule wasn't just for family members; it was for our guests as well.

In all our years of having guests over, no one ever objected to my parents' rule. Why? It was their pool. They built it, they maintained it, and they owned it. People knew intuitively that an owner has the right to make reasonable rules and expect guests to follow them.

The decision to believe or not to believe in God should not be based on preconceptions or on what we want to believe. It ought to be based on evidence, experience and reason. How objective are you about weighing the evidence for and against God?

These five reasons present some strong pointers to the existence of God. I admit it's not a slam-dunk case. But for me, these reasons cause me to conclude that it takes more faith to believe there is no God than to believe that there is. How about you?

1. William Craig, *Reasonable Faith: Christian Truth and Apologetics* (Wheaton, IL: Crossway, 1994), 84.
2. Quoted in *Heroes of History* (W. Frankford, III.: Caleb, 1992), 434.
3. This analogy is adapted from Ray Comfort's *God Doesn't Believe in Atheists* (South Plainfield, NJ: Bridge Publishing, 1993), 15-17.
4. Psalm 139:14, NLT.
5. Jesus made verbal claims to be both Messiah and God. And He made many deliberate non-verbal demonstrations that He was God. See, for instance, Matthew 12:6; 16:16-17; 21:15-16; 23:37; 28:18; Mark 2:1-2; 10:18; 14:53-65; John 4:25-26; 8:58-59.
6. This argument was popularized by Josh McDowell, *A Ready Defense* (Nashville: Thomas Nelson Publishers, 1993) 241-245.
7. C.S. Lewis, *Mere Christianity* (New York: MacMillan Publishing, 1960), 40-41.
8. John 19:1.
9. McDowell, *A Ready Defense*, 222, cites the following expert description: "The heavy whip is brought down with full force again and again across [a person's] shoulders, back and legs…The small balls of lead first produce large, deep bruises, which are broken open by subsequent blows. Finally the skin of the back is hanging in long ribbons and the entire area is an unrecognizable mass of torn, bleeding tissue. When it is determined by the Centurion in charge that the prisoner is near death, the beating is finally stopped."
10. John 19:2.
11. John 19:17.
12. Mark 15:21.
13. John 19:34.
14. Matthew 27:54, NAS.
15. Matthew 27:60; John 19:41.
16. John 19:39.
17. McDowell, *A Ready Defense*, 225.
18. Mark 15:47.
19. Matthew 27:65.
20. Matthew 27:6—A Roman guard unit consisted of 16 men; each was trained to protect the six square feet in front of them. Together they were expected to hold 36 yards against an entire battalion. Four men were stationed directly in front of the object they were protecting, with the other 12 asleep in a fan shape in front of them, with heads pointed in. To pierce this defense, thieves would have to first walk over the sleeping guards, then confront the four fully-armed soldiers. Every four hours a fresh set of four men were awakened and rotated to the direct-guard position.
21. Matthew 27:66.
22. Luke 24:5.

23. Mark 16:11; John 20:13, 20:25.
24. Matthew 27:5.
25. McDowell, *A Ready Defense*, 231.
26. McDowell, *A Ready Defense*, 234. Note: Some people choose to believe that the guards fell asleep or went AWOL. The penalty for either offense was death.
27. John 20:67.
28. Matthew 28:1-6; Mark 16:1-6; Luke 24:1-6; John 20:1.
29. Mark 16:1; Luke 24:13-18, 36-39; John 20:10-18, 19-20, 26-28; 1 Corinthians 15:3-6.
30. Matthew 7:7.
31. Ecclesiastes 3:11, NLT.

Is the Bible True?

IS THE BIBLE TRUE?

"There exists no document from the ancient world witnessed by so excellent a set of textual and historical testimonies, and offering so superb an array of historical data on which an intelligent decision may be made."
Clark Pinnock

People have all kinds of questions about the Bible. One of the most common is, *"With all of the times the Bible has been copied from one language to another, how can we really be sure what it says?"* Whenever that question comes up, my first thought is always, "If you only knew…"

The Bible is the most accurately translated book of all time. Its transmission from one generation to the next has been done so carefully and is so well documented, once people know the whole story they often remark that only God could have done such an excellent job.

The Number of Translations

A common misperception is that the Bible has been translated into so many languages; it must have been translated from one language to another, then to another. Like the child's game of "telephone," where each child whispers into the ear of the next, the message gets progressively garbled as it moves from ear to ear. If the original message was, "The duck is brown," the final message becomes distorted into something like, "Danny loves Susie."

This is why Bible scholars **always translate from the original languages** of Hebrew (99% of the Old Testament), Aramaic (Daniel 2:4-7:28) and Greek (the New Testament), and why they take great pains to ensure that the text of that original Hebrew, Aramaic or Greek is the most reliable version possible.

The Talmudim

The Talmudim (Hebrew for "students") were responsible for the transmission of the Torah (Old Testament) from A.D. 100-500. They had great reverence for the Scriptures in their care, and as a result their process was very careful and precise.

Synagogue scrolls had to be written on specially prepared skins of clean animals and fastened with strings taken from clean animals. Each skin had to contain a certain number of columns. Each column had to have between 48 and 60 lines and be 30 letters wide. The spacing between consonants, sections and books was precise, measured by hairs or threads. The ink had to be black and prepared with a specific recipe. The transcriber could not deviate from the original in any manner. No words could be written from memory. The person making the copy had to wash his whole body before beginning and had to be in full Jewish dress. The scribe had to reverently wipe his pen each time he wrote the word "God" ("Elohim") and wash his whole body before writing God's covenant name "Yahweh."

The Massoretes

The Massoretes, who oversaw the Torah from A.D. 500-900, adopted an even more elaborate means of ensuring transcriptional accuracy. They numbered the verses, words and letters of each book and calculated the midpoint of each one. When a scroll was complete, independent sources counted the number of words and syllables forward, then backward, then from the middle of the text in each direction, to make sure that the exact number had been preserved. Proofreading and revision of a completed manuscript had to be done within 30 days. Up to two mistakes on a page could be corrected. Three mistakes on a page condemned the whole manuscript.

These scribes treated the text so reverently that older manuscripts were destroyed to keep them from being misread. Prior to 1947, the oldest existing Hebrew manuscript was from the ninth century. The discovery of the Dead Sea Scrolls enabled us to check the accuracy of our current Old Testament manuscripts against ones written in approximately 100 B.C. When we compare the 100 B.C. scrolls to our ninth century manuscripts (a 1,000 year gap), we find that an amazing 95% of the texts are identical, with only minor variations. We also have many ancient copies of the Septuagint, the Greek translation of the Old Testament dating from the second century B.C.

New Testament Preservation

The story of the New Testament is equally impressive.

Historians use three criteria to evaluate the reliability of a historical text. They look at 1) the **number** of manuscripts available (the greater the number of manuscripts, the better the ability to compare and reconstruct the original); 2) the **time interval** between the date of original writing and the date the particular manuscript was made (the shorter the time interval, the closer to the actual events and eyewitnesses, and the fewer times the manuscript would have been recopied); and 3) the **quality** of those manuscripts (the more legible the words on the page, the more accurate the reading and comparison with other texts).

So for instance, historians have a high degree of confidence that Julius Caesar conquered Gaul. Why? Because we possess ten ancient manuscripts of Caesar's writings on *The Gallic Wars*. We have a high degree of confidence that Socrates lived, taught and was executed by drinking hemlock. Why? Because we possess seven ancient manuscripts of Plato's *Tetralogies*, in which he documents the death of his beloved mentor and teacher.

Consider the following chart:

Author	When Written	Earliest Copy	Time Span	# of copies
Caesar	100-44 BC	AD 900	1,000 years	10
Plato	427-347 BC	AD 900	1,200 years	7
Tacitus	AD 100	AD 1100	1,000 years	20
Thucydides	460-400 BC	AD 900	1,300 years	8
Aristotle	384-322 BC	AD 1100	1,400 years	49

Of all ancient Greek and Latin literature, Homer's *The Iliad* ranks next to the New Testament in possessing the greatest amount of manuscript testimony.[1] Here is how it compares to the New Testament:

Author	When Written	Earliest Copy	Time Span	# of copies
Homer (Iliad)	900 BC	400 BC	500 years	643
New Testament	AD 40-100	AD 125	25 years	24,000

In terms of quality of manuscripts, author and scholar Ken Boa writes, "While the quality of the Old Testament manuscripts is excellent, that of the New Testament is very good—considerably better than the manuscript quality of other ancient documents."[2]

So What?

By all standards of scholarly accuracy and reliability, the Bible stands head and shoulders above all other literature in history. In the entire New Testament, only 400 words are in question (0.5%). The variants for these words are so slight that no doctrine of Christianity is affected by the differences.

But Is The Bible True?

I have some friends who have an insatiable need for evidence. Theories, hypotheses and even logic don't move these "show-me" types. What they need is factual evidence. God understands that; after all, God was the one who wired them that way. So for my friends and the others like them, there exists tangible evidence for the veracity of the Bible. This evidence comes from not just one source, but three: science, archaeology and prophecy.

Evidence from Science

The Bible is not a scientific textbook. But it does describe how the universe works. Consider the following:[3]

What the Bible says:	What people thought:	What we now know:
Earth is a sphere	Earth is a flat disk	Earth is a sphere
Number of stars = more than a billion	Number of stars = 1,100	Number of stars = more than a billion
Every star is different	All stars are the same	Every star is different
Light is in motion	Light is fixed in place	Light is in motion
Air has weight	Air is weightless	Air has weight
Winds blow in cyclones	Winds blow straight	Winds blow in cyclones
Blood is a source of life and healing	Sick people must be bled	Blood is a source of life and healing

For centuries, scientific theory was at odds with the Genesis 1 description of the physical and biological development of Earth. Today, scientists are in substantial agreement with the initial conditions of Genesis 1 as well as with subsequent events and the order in which they occurred.[4] The likelihood that Moses, writing the first five books of the Bible 3,400 years ago, could have guessed all these details is infinitesimal.

In addition, the Bible describes:

- **The conservation of mass and energy.**[5]

- **The hydraulic cycle of evaporation, condensation and precipitation.**[6]

- **Gravity.**[7]

- **The Pleiades and Orion as gravitationally bound star groups.**[8]

- **The effect of emotions on physical health.**[9]

- **The spread of contagious disease by close contact.**[10]

- **The importance of sanitation to health.**[11]

What grade would you give a book that could do all this and was completed 2,000 years ago?

Astronomer Robert Jastrow sums it up this way: "For the scientist who has lived by his faith in the power of reason, the story ends like a bad dream…he is about to conquer the highest peak [of scientific truth]; as he pulls himself over the final rock, he is greeted by a band of theologians who have been sitting there for centuries."[12]

Evidence from Archaeology

Starting in the late nineteenth century, western scholars began excavating locations throughout the ancient Near East. To date, more than 25,000 sites have been explored.[13] Discoveries from these sites provide a second piece of tangible evidence to support the trustworthiness of the Bible by corroborating Biblical accounts with archeological findings.

Excavations at the cities of Mari, Nuzi and Alalakh verify that Abraham's customs were consistent with his eighteenth century B.C. culture. Excavations at Hazor, Gezer, Megiddo and Jerusalem confirm the account of Joshua's conquest of Canaan, David and Solomon's building of the United Kingdom, the demise of power during the Divided Kingdom and the Babylonian Exile.

One of the more intriguing archeological finds is John Garstang's excavation of the city of Jericho in 1930. Joshua 6:20 indicates the walls of Jericho collapsed in a way that enabled the Israelites to charge straight into the city. For years, skeptics cited this as an example of a Biblical inaccuracy, because city walls do not fall outward; they fall inward when they collapse, leaving the town in

rubble. Guess what Garstang found? The walls fell outward! This finding was so unexpected that he and two other colleagues signed a statement verifying it.[14]

According to the book of John, one of Jesus' great miracles was the healing of the cripple at the Pool of Bethesda[15] (pictured on page 46). Outside of the New Testament, no evidence had ever been found for such a pool, so skeptics pronounced John's writing inaccurate, "the obvious work of an impostor." However, in 1888 traces of the pool were discovered near the church of St. Anne.[16]

Luke, in his gospel, gets very specific with the names of rulers, officials and events, providing ample fodder for criticism. His description of an enrollment of taxpayers,[17] his listing of Quirinius as governor of Syria,[18] his identification of Lystra and Derbe as cities in the province of Lycaonia[19] and his reference to Lysanias as Tetrarch of Abilene[20] were all called into question by Biblical skeptics. However, over time, each of Luke's statements has been verified by archaeological findings.

Archeologist and author Dr. Joseph Free writes, "Archaeology has confirmed countless passages which were rejected by critics as unhistorical or contradictory to known facts."[21]

Evidence from Prophecy

From Moses to Malachi, the role of the prophet was so critical to the well-being of Israel that God wanted His people to know conclusively that these men and women spoke for Him. The Bible lays out a simple test for the authenticity of anyone claiming to be a real prophet of God: 100% accuracy. *"If what a prophet proclaims in the name of the Lord does not take place or come true, that is a message the Lord has not spoken."*[22] *"A prophet who presumes to speak in my name anything I have not commanded…must be put to death."*[23]

So one purpose for the Bible's prophetic predictions is to give people hard evidence that the message being delivered is true. The Bible contains approximately 2,500 prophecies,[24] over 2,000 of which have already been fulfilled.

Can you imagine the boldness of predicting the name and foreign policy of a United States president 150 years from now? In 700 B.C., Isaiah did something similar. He predicted that Jerusalem would be surrounded and its people carried into captivity.[25] That prediction was fulfilled 100 years later. Then he went one step further. He prophesied that the Israelites would return to their homeland, and that the ruler who would set them free would be named Cyrus. "*I will raise up Cyrus in my righteousness... He will rebuild my city and set my exiles free...*"[26] History verifies that Cyrus, the founder of the Persian empire, reigned from 559-530 B.C. and issued a decree in March 538 B.C. that allowed the Jews to return to their homeland.

Ezekiel made an equally startling prediction about the city state of Tyre (in modern day Lebanon).

He prophesied that:

- Many nations would come against Tyre (Ezek. 26:2).

- Nebuchadnezzar would destroy the city (Ezek. 26:4).

- The city would be scraped bare (Ezek. 26:4).

- Fishing nets would be spread over the site (Ezek. 26:5).

- The stones of the city would be thrown into the sea (Ezek. 26:12).

- The city would never be rebuilt (Ezek. 26:14).

Here's what happened: Tyre was a city in two parts. Half the city lay on the coast, the other half on an island one-half mile from shore. The historian Josephus tells us that Nebuchadnezzar besieged the coastal city for 13 years and finally captured it.[27] Many of its citizens escaped to the island, which remained intact.

Then, 240 years later, Alexander the Great attacked the island city.[28] Alexander built a causeway from the mainland to the island, moving the stones and rubble from the old coastal city into the sea to serve as building materials. He literally "scraped away her rubble and made her a bare rock."[29] He also used ships to attack from the sea, ships manned by people from the nations he had already conquered, including 80 from Sidon, Aradus and Byblos; 10 from Rhodes; 10 from Lycia; and 120 from Cyprus.[30] The city of Tyre has never been rebuilt. There is a small town on the island today; fishermen from the town spread and cast their nets from the barren rocks.[31]

The Old Testament contains several hundred prophesies related to the coming Messiah, 332 of which were fulfilled in Christ's first coming.[32] Using the mathematical science of probability, author Peter Stoner, an academic in the areas of science and mathematics, calculated the odds that any one person could fulfill just eight prophesies predicted of the Messiah. After doing his calculations, he said, "...we find that the chance that any man might have lived down to the present time and fulfilled eight prophesies is 1×10^{17}." (1 in 100,000,000,000,000,000.)[33]

To illustrate that in practical terms, Stoner used the following illustration: "Supposing we take 10^{17} silver dollars and lay them on the face of Texas. They will cover all of the state two feet deep. Now mark one of these silver dollars and stir the whole mass thoroughly, all over the state. Blindfold a man and tell him that he can travel as far as he wishes, but he has one chance to pick up a silver dollar and have it be the right one. What are the odds that he will succeed? 1×10^{17}."[34]

Calculating the probability that someone could fulfill 48 prophecies gave Stoner the number 1×10^{157}. The number of atoms in the universe has been calculated at 10^{66}.[35]

1. Bruce Metzger, *Chapters in the History of New Testament Criticism*, (Grand Rapids, MI: Eerdmans, 1964), p. 144.
2. Ken Boa and Larry Moody, *I'm Glad you Asked* (Colorado Springs, CO: Victor Books, 1994), p. 92.
3. Hugh Ross, www.Reasons.org.
4. Source (and for more extensive descriptions, consult) www.Reasons.org.
5. Ecclesiastes 1:9; 3:14-15.
6. Job 36:27-29; Ecclesiastes 1:7; Isaiah 55:10.
7. Job 26:7; Job 38:31-33.
8. Job 38:31 (Note: According to Dr. Ross, "All other star groups visible to the naked eye are unbound, with the possible exception of the Hyades.")
9. Proverbs 15:30; 16:24; 17:22.
10. Leviticus 13:45-46.
11. Numbers 19; Deuteronomy 23:12-13.
12. Robert Jastrow, *The Intellectuals Speak Out About God* (Lake Bluff, IL: Regnery Gateway, 1984), p. 21.
13. Donald Wiseman (Director of the British Museum), "Archaeological Confirmation of the Old Testament," in *Revelation and the Bible*, Carl Henry, editor (Grand Rapids, MI: Baker, 1958), p. 301-2.
14. John Garstang, *Joshua Judges*, 1931, cited in McDowell, *Evidence*, p. 71.
15. John 5:1-15.
16. F.F. Bruce, "Archaeological Confirmation of the New Testament," cited by McDowell, *Evidence*, p. 75.
17. Luke 2:1-2.
18. Luke 2:2.
19. Acts 14:6.
20. Luke 3:1.
21. Joseph Free, *Archaeology and Bible History* (Wheaton: Scripture Press, 1969), p. 1. (As cited in Kumar, *Christianity for Skeptics*, p. 109).
22. Deuteronomy 18:21-22.
23. Deuteronomy 18:20.
24. http://www.iclnet.org/pub/resources/text/rtg/rtg-evid/rtgevd04.txt.
25. Isaiah 27-32.
26. Isaiah 45:13.
27. http://ragz-international.com/chaldeansneb.htm.
28. http://joseph_berrigan.tripod.com/ancientbabylon/id34.html.
29. Ezekiel 26:4.

30. John Ankerberg and John Weldon, *Ready with an Answer* (Eugene, OR: Harvest House, 1997), p. 248.
31. Erwin Lutzer, *You Can Trust the Bible* (Chicago: Moody Press, 1998), p. 98.
32. Floyd Hamilton, *The Basis of the Christian Faith* (New York: Harper and Row, 1964), p. 160, cited in McDowell, *Evidence*, p. 181.
33. Peter Stoner, *Science Speaks* (Chicago: Moody Press, 1963), cited in McDowell, *Evidence*, p. 175-176.
34. Ibid.

Do All Roads Lead to Heaven?

DO ALL ROADS LEAD TO HEAVEN?

> *"To maintain that all religions are paths leading to the same goal...is to maintain something that is not true...The only common ground is that the function of religion is to provide release; there is no agreement at all as to what it is that man must be released from. The great religions are talking at cross purposes."*
>
> R.C. Zaehner

One objection people have to Christianity is that it is too narrow. After all, what kind of a God would limit people to just one way of getting into heaven? Shouldn't He let all well-intentioned people into heaven? Couldn't He be generous and broad-minded enough to let everyone in who tries? Aren't all religions pretty much the same when you get right down to it?

It might surprise you to learn that *every* major religion claims to be the only way to heaven. This chart represents the five largest religions in the world.

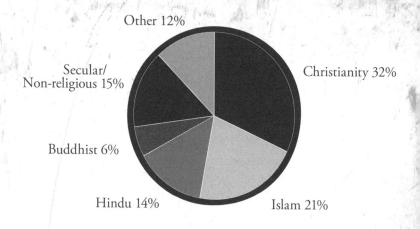

Other 12%

Secular/
Non-religious 15%

Christianity 32%

Buddhist 6%

Hindu 14%

Islam 21%

Let's compare. According to social anthropologists, the top five religions (from smallest to largest) are: Buddhism, Hinduism, "Non-religious," Islam and Christianity. Sociologists lump together all atheists, agnostics and secular people into one "non-religious" religion—and then point out that there are "no truly secular societies." Still, setting these 850 million "non-religious" people aside for the moment leaves us with four religions that teach something about truth, God and/or the afterlife.[1]

#5—Buddhism

Buddhism has roughly 376 million adherents, which equates to about 6% of the world's population. Its founder, Siddhartha Gautama, was born in approximately 563 B.C. to a high caste Hindu family in Nepal. At about the age of 40, Gautama concluded that Hinduism was an inadequate system of belief. So he meditated under a fig tree for 40 days and nights. During this meditation, he became "enlightened," about the nature of life and the means to eternity. For the next 50 years, he was known as "The Buddha," which means "The Enlightened One."

According to Buddhism, God is beyond description. A leading Buddhist scholar claims: "The Buddhist teaching on God, in the sense of an ultimate Reality, is neither agnostic, as is sometimes claimed, nor vague, but clear and logical. Whatever Reality may be, it is beyond the conception of the finite intellect; it follows that attempts at description are misleading, unprofitable, and a waste of time. For these good reasons, the Buddha maintained about Reality, 'a noble silence.'"[2]

During his meditation under the fig tree, the Buddha discovered The Four Noble Truths. These four truths explain the reality of life. (1) **Suffering is universal.** The very act of living brings about pain and suffering. If you are human, you will suffer. (2) **Craving is the root cause of suffering.** If we didn't desire things, we wouldn't feel deprived or lacking or that our lives weren't exactly what we want them to be. (3) **The cure for suffering is to eliminate craving.** And (4) **You eliminate craving by following The Eightfold Path.** The Eightfold Path consists of **right views, right thought, right speech, right behavior, right occupation, right effort, right contemplation** and **right meditation.**

The goal of Buddhism is to be free from pain and suffering. By following his Eightfold Path, The Buddha taught that a person could achieve "enlightenment." Buddhism teaches, "Those who love a hundred have a hundred woes. Those who love ten have ten woes. Those who love one have one woe. Those who love none have no woes."[3] So Buddhism does not so much focus on the afterlife but on this life and the way to overcome suffering, which is to detach yourself from it.

Like the Hinduism from which it sprang, Buddhism believes in Nirvana (which is discussed on page 65) but with a slight twist. Because Buddha saw all life and life forms as temporary, there is no "ultimate place."

According to Buddhism, "…there are six realms of existence into which one can be reborn: as a Hell being, a "hungry" ghost, an animal, a human being, a jealous god and a heavenly being. The most precious of these is seen to be the human birth as this gives the best opportunities for winning enlightenment. A heavenly being is too absorbed in pleasure to think about winning enlightenment. Unlike Christianity, Buddhism sees these states as ultimately temporary. A god, therefore, will eventually descend into one of the lower realms." [4]

#4—Hinduism

Hinduism has roughly 900 million followers today. According to Hindu belief, **Brahman** is the universal spirit, which is everywhere and in everything. It is the unconscious, impersonal force that governs the whole universe. So Hinduism is a **pantheistic** religion. ("Pan" is the Latin word for "all.") Hindus believe that God is in everything. Brahman is the great force, the **circle of life** that ordains everything and puts everything in its place.

Hinduism dates back to 3000 B.C. As ancient Hindus looked around their landscape, they noticed a certain hierarchy to our world. The fish eats the worm, the cat eats the fish, the coyote eats the cat, the mountain lion eats the coyote, the mountain lion gets captured by the game warden and transported to a safer place so that he won't eat the game warden's children. They also noted that even this hierarchy tends to go through a predictable cycle: the game warden dies, is buried in the ground, worms eat his body and the whole thing begins over again. From this, Hindu peoples developed their concept of the road to heaven called, **"the transmigration of souls,"** or reincarnation. They believe that all life has an animating force that inhabits certain physical forms based on its level of goodness, as earned in previous lives.

Here's an example from one of Hinduism's sacred writings:

The murderer of a Brahmin becomes consumptive, the killer of a cow becomes hump-backed and imbecile, the murderer of a virgin becomes leprous—all three born as outcasts. The slayer of a woman and the destroyer of embryos becomes a savage full of diseases; who commits illicit intercourse, a eunuch; who goes with his teacher's wife, disease-skinned. The eater of flesh becomes very red; the drinker of intoxicants, one with discolored teeth…. Who steals food becomes a rat; who steals grain becomes a locust… perfumes, a muskrat; honey, a gadfly; flesh, a vulture; and salt, an ant…. Who commits unnatural vice becomes a village pig; who consorts with a Sudra woman becomes a bull; who is passionate becomes a lustful horse…. These and other signs and births are seen to be the karma of the embodied, made by themselves in this world. Thus the makers of bad karma, having experienced the tortures of Hell, are reborn with the residues of their sins, in these stated forms (Garuda Purana 5).

In the twentieth century, Indian gurus began emigrating to the United States and presenting their teachings on reincarnation. Upwardly mobile, optimistic Americans didn't like the idea that we could regress in our development. The American dream is about more, never less. So when Hinduism came to America, we modified the transmigrational highway, making it run only one way—up. This belief system has become known as "The New Age Movement." The New Age Movement believes in reincarnation, but never in a downward direction. New Age teachers proclaim that we are all gods, and that the god-part of us can't go backwards, only forwards. This belief in purely upward mobility is called "Cosmic Optimism."

The goal of Hindus is to live a life that merits good karma, which will enable them to progress forward on the transmigrational highway in their next life here on earth. If they do this well enough, over time they will advance to the highest level of humanity, which is the caste of Hindu priest called "Brahman." If a Brahman stores up enough karma, eventually he will be elevated out of physical existence into a state of semi-godhood. He'll become a spirit.

If he does very well in that spirit life, he'll be able to advance to the next higher spirit life.

The ultimate goal is to become pure spirit, completely one with the Brahman of the universe. Achieving this state is called "Nirvana," which means "blown away." Because the Hindu's god is an impersonal force that inhabits all things, when people achieve Nirvana they lose all sense of consciousness and become absorbed into the unconsciousness of the universe.

#3—Secularism/Nonreligious/Agnostics/Atheists

Scholars lump these groups together because they all purport to not be interested in religion or spirituality. But one observer notes: "Sociologists point out that there are no truly 'secular' societies… 'nonreligious' people… are those who derive their worldview and value system from alternative, secular, cultural or otherwise nonrevealed systems rather than traditional religious systems."[5]

Many have made the conscious choice not to explore their faith, or at least not publicly. All told, this group numbers about 1.1 billion, or 16% of the world's population.

#2—Islam

Islam is the world's second-largest religion, with some 1.5 billion followers, or 21% of the population. Islam's founder, Mohammed, was born in Mecca near the coast of the Red Sea around A.D. 570. His family was a minor branch of a Bedouin caste of merchant traders called the *"Quraysh."* At that time, the Arab people were polytheists, believing in many gods. According to some sources, they worshiped one god for each day of the year. Allah, the moon god, was one of those. Allah's symbol, the crescent, is still seen as the chief symbol of Islam today.

One night in 610, Mohammed had a visitation from whom he believed was the angel Gabriel. We read in the Koran that the angel told him, "In the name of thy Lord the Creator, who created mankind from a clot of blood, recite!" (Sura 96:1)

Mohammed recited, then described his revelations to his relatives and friends. He taught them that of all the gods they were worshiping, only the one they called "Allah" was the true God and demanded absolute submission to himself. In addition, Mohammed claimed that God had called him as Allah's last and greatest prophet.

The central teaching of Islam indicates the way of submission has Five Pillars:

1. **Recite the shahada.** (*"There is no god but Allah, and Mohammed is his prophet."*)

2. **Pray [salat] five times a day facing Mecca.**

3. **Give [zakat] alms to the poor.**

4. **Fast [sawm] during the month of Ramadan.**

5. **Perform a pilgrimage [hajj] to Mecca at least once.**

Muslims believe that faithfully performing the Five Pillars of the faith will earn them entrance into Paradise. Paradise is a place of celebration and happiness.

According to the Koran:

They shall recline on couches lined with thick brocade, and within reach will hang the fruits of both gardens. Which of the Lord's blessings would you deny? Therein are bashful virgins whom neither man nor jinnee will have touched before. Which of your Lord's blessings would you deny? Virgins as fair as coral and rubies..." (Sura 55:54-60)

Another example:

"They shall recline on jeweled couches face to face, and there shall wait on them immortal youths with bowls and ewers and a cup of purest wine (that will neither pain their heads nor take away their reason); with fruits of their own choice and flesh of fowls that they will relish. And theirs shall be the dark-eyed houris, chaste as hidden pearls: a guerdon [reward] for their deeds." (Sura 56:15-25)

No mention is made of how women benefit from Paradise.

Throughout his lifetime, Mohammed conquered by the sword and commissioned his followers to continue the practice. He said, "Believers, make war on the infidels who dwell around you. Deal firmly with them. Know that God is with the righteous." (Sura 9:123) In at least 18 places in the Koran, Allah commands his followers to fight and kill the enemies of Islam.[6] Sura 5:51 forbids a Muslim to ever take a Jew or Christian as a friend.

#1—Christianity

Christianity believes in grace. Christianity's founder, Jesus Christ, was born in Bethlehem, probably around 4 B.C. At age 30, Jesus began to heal, teach and perform miracles while preparing His disciples to carry on His ministry. In AD April 29, He was crucified, buried and resurrected from the grave[7]. For 40 days He appeared to people before finally ascending into Heaven[8].

Ten days later, the Holy Spirit descended on Jesus' followers, empowering them to preach, heal and perform miracles[9]. The Christian church was born. Today Christianity is the largest religion or organization on earth, with some two billion followers worldwide. It is estimated that as many as 100,000 people become Christians each day.[10]

The Bible says, *"It is not good for a man to be alone."*[11] The dilemma of mankind is that because of our separation from God, we feel alone. To remedy this, every culture in every age has had a belief in God and a desire to be united with Him in some way.

The Bible also says, *"Without the shedding of blood, there is no forgiveness of sins."*[12] In the Bible, blood is shed to pay for sins. Presumed in this is the concept of justice. Justice demands payment when a wrong has occurred. All of us want justice. We don't want to live in a world where God treats Saddam Hussein and Mother Teresa alike. We want things to be fair.

God wants justice too. But, because He is also loving, He wants to give more than justice; He wants to give mercy. How can He be merciful while maintaining justice? By demanding payment, then paying it Himself. That's grace. The Bible describes it this way: *"When the kindness and love of God our Savior appeared, he saved us, not because of the righteous things we had done, but because of his mercy."*[13]

Four Solutions

In Genesis 3, Adam and Eve ate the forbidden fruit, and their sin caused separation from God. For the next eight chapters, God did something very creative: before He gave the **grace solution**, He demonstrated the futility of the solutions that each of the other three major religions will eventually devise.

The Isolation Solution

In Genesis 4, God demonstrates the **isolation solution**. Cain and Abel give offerings to God. Cain's was a half-hearted offering, and God said in effect, "You can do better than that." In his frustration, Cain lashed out and killed his brother. God says, "Cain, from now on, you are going to live in isolation from the rest of the community." He banished Cain from the rest of humanity so that he wouldn't hurt or be hurt by them.

This is the Buddhist solution: withdraw yourself. If you can't be touched, then you can't be hurt. This solution didn't work for Cain. He cried out, *"My punishment is too great for me to bear!"*[14]

The Repetition Solution

God demonstrated the second solution, the **repetition solution**, in Genesis 6. People were doing things to each other that were so hurtful, God caused a giant flood to eliminate all mankind, except the family of Noah. He then started humanity over again with this one ideal family.

This is the solution of Hinduism and the New Age Movement. With enough reincarnations, eventually you will achieve enough good karma to get close to God. The problem? No matter how many chances we get, we're still flawed and finite people, so we continue to make mistakes. This solution didn't work for Noah either; as soon as Noah's children stepped out of the boat, they got into a family feud. Noah gets drunk, one of his sons ridicules him, and Noah cursed the son and all his descendants.[15]

The Exertion Solution

In Genesis 11, on the plains of Babylon, people got together and tried to work their way back to God. They built a tower stretching toward the sky; their plan was to work hard enough to earn their way to heaven. The **exertion solution** is by far the most common response to the problem of aloneness. Islam says, "Work the Five Pillars. Given enough effort, you'll earn your way to Paradise." The Mormons, Jehovah's Witnesses and dozens of other minor religions have all adopted strategies for earning their way to God.

The Relation Solution

After God got through demonstrating the inadequacies of these methods, He began to put His own solution into place. His solution is a relationship based on grace. In Genesis 12, God chose one man, Abraham. He built a relationship with him and began to teach him about grace. He promised that He would turn Abraham into a great nation that would bless "all peoples on earth."[16]

In Exodus 12, God introduced the nation of Israel to the idea of simultaneously fulfilling justice and giving mercy by providing a substitute payment for the people's sins. God said to Moses, *"Tell the whole community of Israel that on the tenth day of this month each man is to take a lamb for his family.... The animals you choose must be year-old males without defect.... Take care of them until the fourteenth day of the month, when all the people of the community of Israel must slaughter them at twilight."*[17] The lamb served as the grace solution for the people. The forfeit of its life served as payment for sin, allowing God to maintain justice while giving grace.

This idea reached its fulfillment in Jesus Christ. On the day Christ began His ministry, John the Baptist declared, *"Behold! The*

Lamb of God who takes away the sin of the world!"[18] For the next three and a half years, Jesus proclaimed that the kingdom of God was at hand. At the end of that time, He was led up a hill to his death, like an innocent lamb to the slaughter. After several hours on the cross, Jesus looked up to heaven and said, *"It is finished."*[19] This was God's solution to man's separation from Him: He enforced justice by taking a life, but the life He took was the life of His Son. God grants forgiveness based on the merits of another.

The Bible says, *"To all who believed him and accept him, he gave the right to become children of God."*[20] In Christianity, instead of asking us to make the effort, God makes the effort for us.

So every person in the world is only one prayer away from heaven. The prayer is a simple request: *"Lord, thank You for what Christ did for me on the Cross. Please accept His sin payment on my behalf and be my Lord."*

The Bible describes heaven as a place in God's presence, where there will be no more tears, death, mourning or pain (Revelation 21). Entrance is granted based on knowing Christ. People from every culture and language will be there (Revelation 7). And everyone will be given responsibilities commensurate with those they assumed for Christ here on earth.[21]

Which Religion Is Right?

Each of these religions has a different kind of God and a vastly different means of reaching Him. Because they're all different, they could all be wrong, but they can't all be right.

Religion	View of God	View of Ultimate Eternity	Way to God
Buddhism	An Impersonal Force	Nirvana	The Eightfold Path
Hinduism	Many gods	Nirvana	Multiple lives and death
Non-religious	None or unknown	None or unknown	None or unknown
Islam	Allah	Paradise	The Five Pillars
Christianity	One God	Heaven	Grace

Many people want to believe that what's most important is the sincerity of a person's faith. "Isn't the sincerity with which I seek God more important than the way I seek Him?" Imagine a skydiver mistakenly reaching for his backpack instead of his parachute just before jumping out of a plane. His well-intentioned error won't help slow his descent to the earth. It is possible to be sincere, but sincerely wrong.

Of the four religions we've considered, three of them (Buddhism, Hinduism and Islam) believe we must practice very specific behavior and follow very specific rules in order to reach their form of heaven. **All of them believe that their "way" is the only way.** Only Christianity teaches that God loved us enough to make the way for us. Only Christianity teaches that God forgives based on His grace, and He opens His arms to us not because of how good we are or how much we do. In some ways, Christianity is the opposite of religion. If religion is about humans reaching up to get to God, Christianity is about God reaching down to us to rescue us. Think about it this way: Buddhism, Hinduism, Islam and all other religions require that you DO certain things in order to make it to their afterlife. Christianity is the only faith system that believes that God has already DONE what is necessary for His children to reach Him.

Since all of these religions are different, we have to make a choice. According to each of these systems, whichever religion you choose will determine your eternity. Which of these systems matches the description of how life seems to work on earth? Which of them offers the most believable description of God? Which of them matches what your heart tells you is true?

1. www.adherents.com.
2. Quoted in Colin Chapman, *Christianity on Trial* (Herts, England: Lion, 1974) p. 226.
3. Cited in Steve Kumar, *Christianity for Skeptics* (Peabody, MA: Hurt Publishing, 2000) p. 129.
4. Anthony Flanagan, "Rebirth" (located at http://buddhism.about.com/library/weekly/aa071602a.htm).
5. www.adherents.com, www.adherents.com/Religions_by_Adherents.html, p. 13.
6. Examples: Sura 2:190, 216; 9:5, 29, 41.
7. 1 Corinthians 15:3.
8. Acts 1:9.
9. Acts 2:1.
10. David Barrett and Todd Johnson's annual report, available at http://www.jesus.org.uk/dawn/2003/dawn16.html and http://gem-werc.org/
11. Genesis 2:18.
12. Hebrews 9:22.
13. Titus 3:5-6.
14. Genesis 4:13.
15. Genesis 9:21-25.
16. Genesis 12:3.
17. Exodus 12:3-6.
18. John 1:29.
19. John 19:30.
20. John 1:12.
21. Matthew 25:23.

How Can a Good God Allow Suffering?

HOW CAN A GOOD GOD ALLOW SUFFERING?

*"God weeps with us so that
we may one day laugh with Him."*
Jürgen Moltmann

The Bible says in John 16:33, *"In this world, you will have trouble."* My personal experience and the daily news broadcasts align with that description. This world is full of trouble.

How do you reconcile a troubled world with a good God? Shouldn't God do something about the trouble? The answer: He is doing something, but we may not be seeing the whole story.

If you have ever opened a novel and started reading at page 100, you know how confusing it can be. The Bible describes the beginning, middle and ending of history. Right now, we're in the middle of history. The whole thing makes much more sense if we can start at the beginning.

In the beginning, God created the heavens and the earth. The earth was a marvelous place; it was paradise. The pinnacle of God's earthly creation was the making of men and women. God

made humans with high reasoning capacity and the ability to make choices for themselves. Another term for the ability to make choices is **free will**.

To understand where suffering comes from, you have to understand free will.

The Option for Evil

In order to offer humankind real freedom, God created us with the ability to choose between right and wrong. In the midst of paradise, God designated one tree and said, *"You are free to eat from any tree in the garden; but you must not eat from the tree of the knowledge of good and evil."*[1]

Like a fish that has always lived in the ocean, Adam and Eve only knew one set of circumstances. A fish may live its whole life without experiencing air (which would be a good thing). But the day it jumps out of the water and takes air into its gills, it begins to understand what water really is.

Similarly, Adam and Eve had no need to know what evil was. But, in order to have free will, God gave them not only the option to choose between a number of good things, but also the option of choosing the evil thing. Evil wasn't God's choice for them (far from it), and He didn't create evil. But He did create the **potential for evil** by designating that one tree as "off-limits". Eventually, they chose to experience the "off-limits" option. Like the fish out of water, from that day forward, they knew what "good" was, because they had experienced its antithesis.

A Perfect World

Many people ask, *"Why didn't God create a world where there was no evil and suffering?"* Answer: He did.

The Bible's opening chapter describes God's creation, from land to plants to fish to birds to animals. Every piece of creation was good. At the end of the full Creation, *"**God saw all that he had made, and it was very good.**"*[2]

Evil and suffering are the result of the choice made by our first parents, Adam and Eve. *"**When Adam sinned, sin entered the entire human race. Adam's sin brought death, so death spread to everyone, for everyone sinned.**"*[3]

Two Kinds of Evil

Human beings experience the effects of their sin, and Creation did as well. The Bible indicates that something damaging happened to the physical universe as a result of Adam and Eve's choice: "*...all creation has been groaning as in the pains of childbirth right up to the present time.*"[4]

This explains natural phenomena that inflict harm on people. When Adam and Eve chose evil, they were telling God that they wanted some space. God honored that choice, and nature was cursed. Genetic breakdown and disease began. Pain and death became part of the human experience. Natural disasters like tornadoes, earthquakes, floods and famines sprang up.

While these "natural" types of calamity occur with regularity, someone has observed that about 95% of all suffering comes from what is called **moral evil**. Moral evil is evil inflicted on one person by another, or by a group of others. When someone dies from a tornado, that's natural evil; when they die from a stab wound, that's moral evil.

Why Would God Let This Happen?

You might ask, *"Why didn't God anticipate this and prevent it?"*

Young couples often wrestle with the potential for birth defects and other dangers as they weigh the decision to have children. Most choose to go ahead in spite of the risks. Why? Because of love, and because of a desire to have a relationship with someone in their own image. God made that same choice.

I Need More

"That's a good answer, but it's not enough for me." Sometimes explanations, even great explanations, aren't enough. This is especially true when the need for explanation flows out of pain. I know this personally.

"Why, God?" is by far the most commonly asked God Question. A young couple asked that question on the day they received the news that their two-month-old daughter had a congenital disease that would cause her much suffering and end her life early.

The little girl wasn't digesting her food well and wasn't growing as fast as others her age. During a routine check-up, her mother asked the doctor if something might be wrong.

The unfortunate result of the test was summed up by the doctor, "Your daughter has cystic fibrosis."

The gene that causes this illness is recessive, so both parents must be carriers to pass it on. Neither the father nor mother knew of anyone in their family who had ever had the disease. Yet here it was. The little girl, Marcia, was my older sister.

Growing up, there was never a morning when Marcia didn't have to take a special pill to help her digest her food properly. By the time she was eight years old, her nightly routine included spending two hours with her head below her chest and my mom patting on her back to loosen the phlegm in her lungs.

By age ten, Marcia's condition had weakened her to the point where she spent at least two weeks a year in the hospital fighting pneumonia. At age twelve, she was sleeping in an oxygen tent at night. When Marcia was sixteen, Dad moved out. I later learned that 85% of parents of children with cystic fibrosis divorce. The constant strain, pressure and financial drain are more than most marriages can endure. The most haunting memory of my young life came a year later when Marcia died. I heard the muffled sobs of my mother in her bedroom, grieving the loss of the child she had loved and cared for so dearly.

Only one question was on my mind that night: "Why, God? Why?"

Two Kinds of Answers

I know my mother's pain. I watched it up close. But my father was more private about his suffering. Although he was raised in a religious home, his little girl's suffering raised questions beyond what his huge intellect could bear. Decades later, he remains unwilling to believe in a God who is all-knowing, all-powerful and all-loving, because he is unable to accept that such a God could sit back and do nothing while one of His children suffered so much.

When it comes to the question of suffering, there are two kinds of answers. One kind helps us understand—these are **logic-based answers**. A second kind helps us emotionally—these are **feeling-based answers**. Most people in pain have a hard time listening to logic. What they need first is something that touches their heart.

During the week I was writing this, a young man named Steve shared his story with our church. He arrived home one day to find

the house empty, with a message that he was to join the family at the hospital. Upon entering the Emergency Room, he was greeted by the news that his father and brother had died in a traffic accident. A younger brother survived, but lost 1/3 of his brain. In the 14 years since that accident, his brother endured 20 surgeries.

Steve loves God passionately. He serves on our vocal team, and his wife is part of our paid staff. But understandably, Steve has struggled deeply with trusting God after the loss of his father and brother. In moments of desperation, he has even considered taking his own life. His pain was and continues to be very real. But so is his faith. What has given Steve the resolve to continue to trust God? Two things: **compassion** and **community**.

During the dark night of his soul, members of his family and church wrapped their arms around him. He knew they cared. He experienced their compassion and community. More importantly, the answers Steve received spoke not only to his mind but to his **emotions**.

Steve knows from experience the story of Christ's suffering on behalf of the sins of the world.

When we hurt, it is almost impossible to believe in a God who gave us enough free will to get ourselves into the mess we're in. While the answer of "free will" makes sense, it's not emotionally satisfying. When we hurt, we need to be touched emotionally, not just intellectually.

Steve knew that Christ had given the ultimate feeling-based answer to the problem of pain: He endured it Himself. When the question, "How could God put anyone through this much pain?" came to Steve, the answer was always, "This pain was not of God's doing, but He willingly suffered this level of pain, and more, for you."

In the midst of his pain, Steve was touched by God's love—the deep love of a Father who not only says, "I am so sorry," but also says, "I know exactly how you feel."

When I hurt, I don't want logic, because I'm too numb to care that God is all-knowing and all-powerful. But I am touched by His love, a love that is so genuine it chose to suffer for me. I can respond to a God like that.

The answer that Steve needed was God's compassion. For most people who have been deeply wounded, knowing that there are intellectual answers, like the problem of free will, helps us a little.

But experiencing His compassion through the love of Christ and the community of others heals us a lot.

I believe there were hints of God's compassion all over my sister's life and death. She was endowed with outstanding gifts and an astounding spirit. Everyone who knew her loved her. And, while I'm not sure about this, sometimes I wonder if the shortened span of her painful life was a gift from God. For the Bible says, *"No eye has seen, no ear has heard, no mind has conceived what God has prepared for those who love him."*[5]

Rather than suffer in her diseased body for these last three decades, Marcia has been experiencing wonders I cannot yet begin to comprehend. I can believe in a God like that, because He demonstrated His compassion to me through His Son and the community of His church.

The Full Story

The story of the world is the story of God and His perfect Creation, which allowed for the possibility of evil and suffering by granting freedom of choice to His children. We chose to experience the evil and suffering. If you think of the history of our world as a three-act play, that's Act I.

God then chose to make provision for our wrong choices by sending His Son to pay the penalty for them. That's Act II. This payment is available to all who will admit their need for it and trust Christ.

Because of the destructive power of evil, God will one day say, "Enough!" He will judge the world, separating sin, evil and death from all that is good and from all who have been forgiven by trusting in Christ. This will initiate Act III. Paradise will be fully restored in what the Bible calls *"the new heaven and the new earth,"* in *"…a world where everyone is right with God."*[6]

The Best Part

The best part of the story is that all the pain and suffering of this world will seem insignificant compared to the pleasure we will experience in heaven. Most of us have had our share of bumps and bruises in this life. Compare yours to those of the Apostle Paul:

> *"I have worked harder, been put in jail more often, been whipped times without number, and faced death again and again. Five different times the Jews gave me thirty-nine lashes. Three times I was beaten with rods. Once I was stoned."*[7]

Yet, in the same letter, when Paul thinks about what he will experience in the life to come, he says, *"Our present troubles are quite small and won't last very long. Yet they produce for us an immeasurably great glory that will last forever!"*[8] Suppose on the first day of this year, you had a terrible day. You woke up with a migraine headache. The pain was so bad that you were afraid you were going to die. Then it got so bad that you wanted to die. On the way to the doctor's office, you were hit by an uninsured motorist, totaling your car. The car was a Christmas present, and it was the car you had always dreamed of owning. You found out your company was downsizing, and your name was at the top of the list. The whole day was like that—terrible. Then, the next day, you woke up to a phone call from a competitor, offering you a better job with twice the pay.

Suppose the entire rest of the year turns out to be like day two? You inherit $1,000,000 from an unknown relative. You buy a lottery ticket with the first dollar, and you win another $10,000,000! Your children earn straight A's. They are so good, their teachers ask to take you to dinner because they want to meet the parent of such outstanding children. Your marriage is perfect. You get voted "Person of the Year" by the local newspaper. You play golf with Tiger Woods—and you win! On December 31, someone asks you, "So, how was your year?"

"It was unbelievable!"

"Really? How about that first day?"

"Oh, yeah, that was a little rough, but everything else has gone so well, I had almost forgotten about it."

That's what it will be like in heaven.[9] That's Act III.

1. Genesis 2:16-17.
2. Genesis 1:31.
3. Romans 5:12, NLT.
4. Romans 8:22, NLT.
5. 1 Corinthians 2:9.
6. 2 Peter 3:13.
7. 2 Corinthians 11:23-27, NLT.
8. 2 Corinthians 4:17, NLT.
9. We are indebted to a sermon by Lee Strobel for this concept.

What Do I Do Now?

WHAT DO I DO NOW?

As you come to the close of a book like this, you can respond in one of two ways. Some people say, "I finished the book; what will I read next?"

Others have a different response. They say, "I've learned some new things; what am I going to do about it?" I hope you'll choose the bold way, because with what you've learned, a whole new world stands before you.

Here are five suggestions for the first steps in your new adventure:

Receive Christ

Today can be your day of salvation. The Bible says, *"To all who received him, to those who believed in his name, he gave the right to become children of God..."*[1] Because Jesus already paid the price for your sins, all you have to do is acknowledge that He did so and invite Him to apply that payment to your life. If you haven't already done so, you can receive His grace and forgiveness right now by praying a simple prayer like this: *"Lord Jesus, I believe in*

You. I receive You now into my life. I want to be a Christian. Forgive me for the things I have done wrong. Lead me from now on." Why not say those words to Him right now?

If you prayed that prayer, all the promises of God, and all the truths of this book, will be applied to your life—starting this very moment! The Bible says, ***"There is rejoicing in the presence of the angels of God over one sinner who repents."***[2]

Get More Answers

If you feel you need more answers to your questions, the full version of *The God Questions* provides 40 days of readings that address many more questions than are covered here. Other resources are available at www.halseed.com.

Become Part of a Local Church

Spiritual growth happens best in community with others. If you're not already attending one, find a church near your home where the Bible is taught and the people are friendly. You'll find that attending church every week is like resetting your clock: it dials in your priorities and reminds you of what's really important. A good weekly church service can inspire you to love God and live your life at the highest level; it's essential for deepening your relationship with God and growing as a person of character and faith. You may be tempted to think, *"I don't have time for church,"* but studies show that people who attend church regularly (at least three out of four weekends per month) live longer than those who don't—so church attendance will actually buy you more time in the long run!

Take Personal Responsibility for Your Spiritual Growth

Every athlete knows that he or she must train in order to improve. The Bible and prayer are the two best tools for spiritual training. Find a Bible and begin reading a chapter or two per day while asking the question, *"What is God saying to me here?"* (This may be the best God Question of all.) Then spend a few minutes talking to Him about your life and the part you want Him to play in it. These two practices will help you more than anything else to become the person you and God want you to be.

Share What You've Learned

One of the greatest acts of love is to share that which will help others. In the next few days, look for opportunities to share what you've learned from *The God Questions*. If it's appropriate, you might give copies of this book to your friends and offer to take them to coffee after they've read it. These conversations might be some of the most meaningful ones you'll ever have.

1. John 1:12.
2. Luke 15:16.

Want More Information?

WANT MORE INFORMATION?

If you've enjoyed this Gift Edition and want more information, you can find it in the full version of *The God Questions*. The full version includes some of the information you've just read, along with additional discussion on questions like:

- What happens to me when I die?

- What's the purpose of the church?

- What's the purpose of my life?

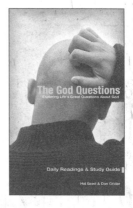

The God Questions provides additional detail and discussion on the four major questions covered in the Gift Edition. The book is formatted with 37 days of devotional reading plus weekly small group discussion questions, so you can share *The God Questions* with friends and family in a group setting.

Look for *The God Questions* at your local Christian bookstore or visit Outreach.com.

WE'D LIKE TO HEAR FROM YOU

We published *The God Questions* Gift Edition to help people with their spiritual journey. If this book (or a particular chapter) has helped you, we would love to hear your story!

Also, if you have questions, we would be happy to connect you with people and resources that can help you find answers.

Please send your comments and experiences with *The God Questions* Gift Edition to us through the "Contact Us" button at www.halseedbooks.com. The website also has articles, additional resources and a blog you might enjoy.

ADDITIONAL BOOKS FROM THE AUTHOR

Future History: Understanding the Book of Daniel and End Times Prophecy

Future History is a perfect resource for any Bible study focusing on the passion of Daniel—his visions and adventures. Immerse yourself in some of the Bible's most-loved stories like The Lions' Den, The Fiery Furnace and the Handwriting on the Wall.

In addition to unpacking the future, Hal draws life lessons out of every chapter of Daniel. *Future History* not only helps you understand what's coming, but its principles for living will help you live a better life now.

To learn more, read a sample chapter, or review other books, CDs and resources from Hal Seed, visit www.halseedbooks.com.

ADDITIONAL BOOKS FROM THE AUTHOR

Jonah: Responding to God in All the Right Ways

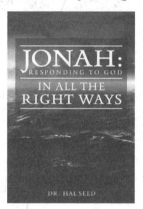

In the story of Jonah, everyone and everything responds to God in amazing ways—except Jonah. Find out how to respond to a God who is both great and gracious to winds and waves, sailors and Ninevites, and even to a wayward prophet.

To learn more, read a sample chapter, or review other books, CDs and resources from Hal Seed, visit www.halseedbooks.com.

WITH GRATITUDE TO:

Scott Evans, for his inspiration to make this gift edition possible;
Jennifer Dion, for excellent insights and editing;
Toni Ridgaway, for editing and attention to details;
Alexia Wuerdeman, for design and graphics;
Dan Grider, for authoring *The God Questions* with me;
And so many pastors and Christian leaders who have helped people
discover answers to their questions about God.

Books are rarely the product of just one person's efforts—it takes a village!

ABOUT THE AUTHOR

Dr. Hal Seed pastors New Song Community Church in Oceanside, CA, one of the most innovative and evangelistically effective churches of our day. Hal and his wife Lori have two children, Bryan and Amy, and love helping people find answers to their questions about God. Hal speaks widely on leadership, church planting, personal growth and evangelism. He also writes books that help pastors reach their communities. You can reach him through www.halseedbooks.com.